This planner belongs to:

Thank yo so much for choosing our planners!
Your voice really matters,
so please don't hesitate to leave us a rating or review.

massy planners

Full Year at a Glance 2023

January

S	M	T	W	T	F	S
1	2	3	4	5	6	7
8	9	10	11	12	13	14
15	16	17	18	19	20	21
22	23	24	25	26	27	28
29	30	31				

February

S	M	T	W	T	F	S
			1	2	3	4
5	6	7	8	9	10	11
12	13	14	15	16	17	18
19	20	21	22	23	24	25
26	27	28				

March

S	M	T	W	T	F	S
			1	2	3	4
5	6	7	8	9	10	11
12	13	14	15	16	17	18
19	20	21	22	23	24	25
26	27	28	29	30	31	

April

S	M	T	W	T	F	S
						1
2	3	4	5	6	7	8
9	10	11	12	13	14	15
16	17	18	19	20	21	22
23	24	25	26	27	28	29
30						

May

S	M	T	W	T	F	S
	1	2	3	4	5	6
7	8	9	10	11	12	13
14	15	16	17	18	19	20
21	22	23	24	25	26	27
28	29	30	31			

June

S	M	T	W	T	F	S
				1	2	3
4	5	6	7	8	9	10
11	12	13	14	15	16	17
18	19	20	21	22	23	24
25	26	27	28	29	30	

July

S	M	T	W	T	F	S
						1
2	3	4	5	6	7	8
9	10	11	12	13	14	15
16	17	18	19	20	21	22
23	24	25	26	27	28	29
30	31					

August

S	M	T	W	T	F	S
		1	2	3	4	5
6	7	8	9	10	11	12
13	14	15	16	17	18	19
20	21	22	23	24	25	26
27	28	29	30	31		

September

S	M	T	W	T	F	S
					1	2
3	4	5	6	7	8	9
10	11	12	13	14	15	16
17	18	19	20	21	22	23
24	25	26	27	28	29	30

October

S	M	T	W	T	F	S
1	2	3	4	5	6	7
8	9	10	11	12	13	14
15	16	17	18	19	20	21
22	23	24	25	26	27	28
29	30	31				

November

S	M	T	W	T	F	S
			1	2	3	4
5	6	7	8	9	10	11
12	13	14	15	16	17	18
19	20	21	22	23	24	25
26	27	28	29	30		

December

S	M	T	W	T	F	S
					1	2
3	4	5	6	7	8	9
10	11	12	13	14	15	16
17	18	19	20	21	22	23
24	25	26	27	28	29	30
31						

Important Dates

January

February

March

April

May

June

July

August

September

October

November

December

Birthdays

January	February	March
April	May	June
July	August	September
October	November	December

Projects / Goals / Notes

January 2023

SUNDAY	MONDAY	TUESDAY	WEDNESDAY	THURSDAY
1	2	3	4	5
8	9	10	11	12
15	16	17	18	19
22	23	24	25	26
29	30	31		

2023

FRIDAY	SATURDAY
6	7
13	14
20	21
27	28

January

SU	MO	TU	WE	TH	FR	SA
1	2	3	4	5	6	7
8	9	10	11	12	13	14
15	16	17	18	19	20	21
22	23	24	25	26	27	28
29	30	31				

Goals / To Do List

Notes

February 2023

SUNDAY	MONDAY	TUESDAY	WEDNESDAY	THURSDAY
			1	2
5	6	7	8	9
12	13	14	15	16
19	20	21	22	23
26	27	28		

2023

FRIDAY	SATURDAY
3	4
10	11
17	18
24	25

February

SU	MO	TU	WE	TH	FR	SA
			1	2	3	4
5	6	7	8	9	10	11
12	13	14	15	16	17	18
19	20	21	22	23	24	25
26	27	28				

Goals / To Do List

Notes

March 2023

SUNDAY	MONDAY	TUESDAY	WEDNESDAY	THURSDAY
			1	2
5	6	7	8	9
12	13	14	15	16
19	20	21	22	23
26	27	28	29	30

2023

FRIDAY	SATURDAY
3	4
10	11
17	18
24	25
31	

March

SU	MO	TU	WE	TH	FR	SA
			1	2	3	4
5	6	7	8	9	10	11
12	13	14	15	16	17	18
19	20	21	22	23	24	25
26	27	28	29	30	31	

Goals / To Do List

Notes

April 2023

SUNDAY	MONDAY	TUESDAY	WEDNESDAY	THURSDAY
30				
2	3	4	5	6
9	10	11	12	13
16	17	18	19	20
23	24	25	26	27

2023

FRIDAY	SATURDAY
	1
7	8
14	15
21	22
28	29

April

SU	MO	TU	WE	TH	FR	SA
						1
2	3	4	5	6	7	8
9	10	11	12	13	14	15
16	17	18	19	20	21	22
23	24	25	26	27	28	29
30						

Goals / To Do List

Notes

May 2023

SUNDAY	MONDAY	TUESDAY	WEDNESDAY	THURSDAY
	1	2	3	4
7	8	9	10	11
14	15	16	17	18
21	22	23	24	25
28	29	30	31	

2023

FRIDAY	SATURDAY
5	6
12	13
19	20
26	27

May

SU	MO	TU	WE	TH	FR	SA
	1	2	3	4	5	6
7	8	9	10	11	12	13
14	15	16	17	18	19	20
21	22	23	24	25	26	27
28	29	30	31			

Goals / To Do List

- ○ ______
- ○ ______
- ○ ______
- ○ ______
- ○ ______
- ○ ______
- ○ ______
- ○ ______
- ○ ______
- ○ ______
- ○ ______

Notes

June 2023

SUNDAY	MONDAY	TUESDAY	WEDNESDAY	THURSDAY
				1
4	5	6	7	8
11	12	13	14	15
18	19	20	21	22
25	26	27	28	29

2023

FRIDAY	SATURDAY
2	3
9	10
16	17
23	24
30	

June

SU	MO	TU	WE	TH	FR	SA
				1	2	3
4	5	6	7	8	9	10
11	12	13	14	15	16	17
18	19	20	21	22	23	24
25	26	27	28	29	30	

Goals / To Do List

Notes

July 2023

SUNDAY	MONDAY	TUESDAY	WEDNESDAY	THURSDAY
30	31			
2	3	4	5	6
9	10	11	12	13
16	17	18	19	20
23	24	25	26	27

2023

FRIDAY	SATURDAY
	1
7	8
14	15
21	22
28	29

July

SU	MO	TU	WE	TH	FR	SA
						1
2	3	4	5	6	7	8
9	10	11	12	13	14	15
16	17	18	19	20	21	22
23	24	25	26	27	28	29
30	31					

Goals / To Do List

- ○
- ○
- ○
- ○
- ○
- ○
- ○
- ○
- ○
- ○
- ○

Notes

August 2023

SUNDAY	MONDAY	TUESDAY	WEDNESDAY	THURSDAY
		1	2	3
6	7	8	9	10
13	14	15	16	17
20	21	22	23	24
27	28	29	30	31

2023

FRIDAY	SATURDAY
4	5
11	12
18	19
25	26

August

SU	MO	TU	WE	TH	FR	SA
		1	2	3	4	5
6	7	8	9	10	11	12
13	14	15	16	17	18	19
20	21	22	23	24	25	26
27	28	29	30	31		

Goals / To Do List

- ○ ___
- ○ ___
- ○ ___
- ○ ___
- ○ ___
- ○ ___
- ○ ___
- ○ ___
- ○ ___
- ○ ___
- ○ ___

Notes

September 2023

SUNDAY	MONDAY	TUESDAY	WEDNESDAY	THURSDAY
3	4	5	6	7
10	11	12	13	14
17	18	19	20	21
24	25	26	27	28

2023

FRIDAY	SATURDAY
1	2
8	9
15	16
22	23
29	30

September

SU	MO	TU	WE	TH	FR	SA
					1	2
3	4	5	6	7	8	9
10	11	12	13	14	15	16
17	18	19	20	21	22	23
24	25	26	27	28	29	30

Goals / To Do List

Notes

October 2023

SUNDAY	MONDAY	TUESDAY	WEDNESDAY	THURSDAY
1	2	3	4	5
8	9	10	11	12
15	16	17	18	19
22	23	24	25	26
29	30	31		

2023

FRIDAY	SATURDAY
6	7
13	14
20	21
27	28

October

SU	MO	TU	WE	TH	FR	SA
1	2	3	4	5	6	7
8	9	10	11	12	13	14
15	16	17	18	19	20	21
22	23	24	25	26	27	28
29	30	31				

Goals / To Do List

Notes

November 2023

SUNDAY	MONDAY	TUESDAY	WEDNESDAY	THURSDAY
			1	2
5	6	7	8	9
12	13	14	15	16
19	20	21	22	23
26	27	28	29	30

2023

FRIDAY	SATURDAY
3	4
10	11
17	18
24	25

November

SU	MO	TU	WE	TH	FR	SA
			1	2	3	4
5	6	7	8	9	10	11
12	13	14	15	16	17	18
19	20	21	22	23	24	25
26	27	28	29	30		

Goals / To Do List

Notes

December 2023

SUNDAY	MONDAY	TUESDAY	WEDNESDAY	THURSDAY
31				
3	4	5	6	7
10	11	12	13	14
17	18	19	20	21
24	25	26	27	28

2023

FRIDAY	SATURDAY
1	2
8	9
15	16
22	23
29	30

December

SU	MO	TU	WE	TH	FR	SA
					1	2
3	4	5	6	7	8	9
10	11	12	13	14	15	16
17	18	19	20	21	22	23
24	25	26	27	28	29	30
31						

Goals / To Do List

Notes

NOTES

NOTES

NOTES

NOTES

Full Year at a Glance 2024

January

S	M	T	W	T	F	S
	1	2	3	4	5	6
7	8	9	10	11	12	13
14	15	16	17	18	19	20
21	22	23	24	25	26	27
28	29	30	31			

February

S	M	T	W	T	F	S
				1	2	3
4	5	6	7	8	9	10
11	12	13	14	15	16	17
18	19	20	21	22	23	24
25	26	27	28	29		

March

S	M	T	W	T	F	S
					1	2
3	4	5	6	7	8	9
10	11	12	13	14	15	16
17	18	19	20	21	22	23
24	25	26	27	28	29	30
31						

April

S	M	T	W	T	F	S
	1	2	3	4	5	6
7	8	9	10	11	12	13
14	15	16	17	18	19	20
21	22	23	24	25	26	27
28	29	30				

May

S	M	T	W	T	F	S
			1	2	3	4
5	6	7	8	9	10	11
12	13	14	15	16	17	18
19	20	21	22	23	24	25
26	27	28	29	30	31	

June

S	M	T	W	T	F	S
						1
2	3	4	5	6	7	8
9	10	11	12	13	14	15
16	17	18	19	20	21	22
23	24	25	26	27	28	29
30						

July

S	M	T	W	T	F	S
	1	2	3	4	5	6
7	8	9	10	11	12	13
14	15	16	17	18	19	20
21	22	23	24	25	26	27
28	29	30	31			

August

S	M	T	W	T	F	S
				1	2	3
4	5	6	7	8	9	10
11	12	13	14	15	16	17
18	19	20	21	22	23	24
25	26	27	28	29	30	31

September

S	M	T	W	T	F	S
1	2	3	4	5	6	7
8	9	10	11	12	13	14
15	16	17	18	19	20	21
22	23	24	25	26	27	28
29	30					

October

S	M	T	W	T	F	S
		1	2	3	4	5
6	7	8	9	10	11	12
13	14	15	16	17	18	19
20	21	22	23	24	25	26
27	28	29	30	31		

November

S	M	T	W	T	F	S
					1	2
3	4	5	6	7	8	9
10	11	12	13	14	15	16
17	18	19	20	21	22	23
24	25	26	27	28	29	30

December

S	M	T	W	T	F	S
1	2	3	4	5	6	7
8	9	10	11	12	13	14
15	16	17	18	19	20	21
22	23	24	25	26	27	28
29	30	31				

Important Dates

January

February

March

April

May

June

July

August

September

October

November

December

Birthdays

January	February	March
April	**May**	**June**
July	**August**	**September**
October	**November**	**December**

Projects / Goals / Notes

January 2024

SUNDAY	MONDAY	TUESDAY	WEDNESDAY	THURSDAY
	1	2	3	4
7	8	9	10	11
14	15	16	17	18
21	22	23	24	25
28	29	30	31	

2024

FRIDAY	SATURDAY
5	6
12	13
19	20
26	27

January

SU	MO	TU	WE	TH	FR	SA
	1	2	3	4	5	6
7	8	9	10	11	12	13
14	15	16	17	18	19	20
21	22	23	24	25	26	27
28	29	30	31			

Goals / To Do List

Notes

February 2024

SUNDAY	MONDAY	TUESDAY	WEDNESDAY	THURSDAY
				1
4	5	6	7	8
11	12	13	14	15
18	19	20	21	22
25	26	27	28	29

2024

FRIDAY	SATURDAY
2	3
9	10
16	17
23	24

February

SU	MO	TU	WE	TH	FR	SA
				1	2	3
4	5	6	7	8	9	10
11	12	13	14	15	16	17
18	19	20	21	22	23	24
25	26	27	28	29		

Goals / To Do List

Notes

March 2024

SUNDAY	MONDAY	TUESDAY	WEDNESDAY	THURSDAY
31				
3	4	5	6	7
10	11	12	13	14
17	18	19	20	21
24	25	26	27	28

2024

FRIDAY	SATURDAY
1	2
8	9
15	16
22	23
29	30

March

SU	MO	TU	WE	TH	FR	SA
					1	2
3	4	5	6	7	8	9
10	11	12	13	14	15	16
17	18	19	20	21	22	23
24	25	26	27	28	29	30
31						

Goals / To Do List

Notes

April 2024

SUNDAY	MONDAY	TUESDAY	WEDNESDAY	THURSDAY
	1	2	3	4
7	8	9	10	11
14	15	16	17	18
21	22	23	24	25
28	29	30		

2024

FRIDAY	SATURDAY
5	6
12	13
19	20
26	27

April

SU	MO	TU	WE	TH	FR	SA
	1	2	3	4	5	6
7	8	9	10	11	12	13
14	15	16	17	18	19	20
21	22	23	24	25	26	27
28	29	30				

Goals / To Do List

Notes

May 2024

SUNDAY	MONDAY	TUESDAY	WEDNESDAY	THURSDAY
			1	2
5	6	7	8	9
12	13	14	15	16
19	20	21	22	23
26	27	28	29	30

2024

FRIDAY	SATURDAY
3	4
10	11
17	18
24	25
31	

May

SU	MO	TU	WE	TH	FR	SA
			1	2	3	4
5	6	7	8	9	10	11
12	13	14	15	16	17	18
19	20	21	22	23	24	25
26	27	28	29	30	31	

Goals / To Do List

Notes

June 2024

SUNDAY	MONDAY	TUESDAY	WEDNESDAY	THURSDAY
30				
2	3	4	5	6
9	10	11	12	13
16	17	18	19	20
23	24	25	26	27

2024

FRIDAY	SATURDAY
	1
7	8
14	15
21	22
28	29

June

SU	MO	TU	WE	TH	FR	SA
						1
2	3	4	5	6	7	8
9	10	11	12	13	14	15
16	17	18	19	20	21	22
23	24	25	26	27	28	29
30						

Goals / To Do List

Notes

July 2024

SUNDAY	MONDAY	TUESDAY	WEDNESDAY	THURSDAY
	1	2	3	4
7	8	9	10	11
14	15	16	17	18
21	22	23	24	25
28	29	30	31	

2024

FRIDAY	SATURDAY
5	6
12	13
19	20
26	27

July

SU	MO	TU	WE	TH	FR	SA
	1	2	3	4	5	6
7	8	9	10	11	12	13
14	15	16	17	18	19	20
21	22	23	24	25	26	27
28	29	30	31			

Goals / To Do List

Notes

August 2024

SUNDAY	MONDAY	TUESDAY	WEDNESDAY	THURSDAY
				1
4	5	6	7	8
11	12	13	14	15
18	19	20	21	22
25	26	27	28	29

2024

FRIDAY	SATURDAY
2	3
9	10
16	17
23	24
30	31

August

SU	MO	TU	WE	TH	FR	SA
				1	2	3
4	5	6	7	8	9	10
11	12	13	14	15	16	17
18	19	20	21	22	23	24
25	26	27	28	29	30	31

Goals / To Do List

Notes

September 2024

SUNDAY	MONDAY	TUESDAY	WEDNESDAY	THURSDAY
1	2	3	4	5
8	9	10	11	12
15	16	17	18	19
22	23	24	25	26
29	30			

2024

FRIDAY	SATURDAY
6	7
13	14
20	21
27	28

September

SU	MO	TU	WE	TH	FR	SA
1	2	3	4	5	6	7
8	9	10	11	12	13	14
15	16	17	18	19	20	21
22	23	24	25	26	27	28
29	30					

Goals / To Do List

Notes

October 2024

SUNDAY	MONDAY	TUESDAY	WEDNESDAY	THURSDAY
		1	2	3
6	7	8	9	10
13	14	15	16	17
20	21	22	23	24
27	28	29	30	31

2024

FRIDAY	SATURDAY
4	5
11	12
18	19
25	26

October

SU	MO	TU	WE	TH	FR	SA
		1	2	3	4	5
6	7	8	9	10	11	12
13	14	15	16	17	18	19
20	21	22	23	24	25	26
27	28	29	30	31		

Goals / To Do List

Notes

November 2024

SUNDAY	MONDAY	TUESDAY	WEDNESDAY	THURSDAY
3	4	5	6	7
10	11	12	13	14
17	18	19	20	21
24	25	26	27	28

2024

FRIDAY	SATURDAY
1	2
8	9
15	16
22	23
29	30

November

SU	MO	TU	WE	TH	FR	SA
					1	2
3	4	5	6	7	8	9
10	11	12	13	14	15	16
17	18	19	20	21	22	23
24	25	26	27	28	29	30

Goals / To Do List

Notes

December 2024

SUNDAY	MONDAY	TUESDAY	WEDNESDAY	THURSDAY
1	2	3	4	5
8	9	10	11	12
15	16	17	18	19
22	23	24	25	26
29	30	31		

2024

FRIDAY	SATURDAY
6	7
13	14
20	21
27	28

December

SU	MO	TU	WE	TH	FR	SA
1	2	3	4	5	6	7
8	9	10	11	12	13	14
15	16	17	18	19	20	21
22	23	24	25	26	27	28
29	30	31				

Goals / To Do List

Notes

NOTES

NOTES

NOTES

NOTES

Full Year at a Glance 2025

January

S	M	T	W	T	F	S
			1	2	3	4
5	6	7	8	9	10	11
12	13	14	15	16	17	18
19	20	21	22	23	24	25
26	27	28	29	30	31	

February

S	M	T	W	T	F	S
						1
2	3	4	5	6	7	8
9	10	11	12	13	14	15
16	17	18	19	20	21	22
23	24	25	26	27	28	

March

S	M	T	W	T	F	S
						1
2	3	4	5	6	7	8
9	10	11	12	13	14	15
16	17	18	19	20	21	22
23	24	25	26	27	28	29
30	31					

April

S	M	T	W	T	F	S
		1	2	3	4	5
6	7	8	9	10	11	12
13	14	15	16	17	18	19
20	21	22	23	24	25	26
27	28	29	30			

May

S	M	T	W	T	F	S
				1	2	3
4	5	6	7	8	9	10
11	12	13	14	15	16	17
18	19	20	21	22	23	24
25	26	27	28	29	30	31

June

S	M	T	W	T	F	S
1	2	3	4	5	6	7
8	9	10	11	12	13	14
15	16	17	18	19	20	21
22	23	24	25	26	27	28
29	30					

July

S	M	T	W	T	F	S
		1	2	3	4	5
6	7	8	9	10	11	12
13	14	15	16	17	18	19
20	21	22	23	24	25	26
27	28	29	30	31		

August

S	M	T	W	T	F	S
					1	2
3	4	5	6	7	8	9
10	11	12	13	14	15	16
17	18	19	20	21	22	23
24	25	26	27	28	29	30
31						

September

S	M	T	W	T	F	S
	1	2	3	4	5	6
7	8	9	10	11	12	13
14	15	16	17	18	19	20
21	22	23	24	25	26	27
28	29	30				

October

S	M	T	W	T	F	S
			1	2	3	4
5	6	7	8	9	10	11
12	13	14	15	16	17	18
19	20	21	22	23	24	25
26	27	28	29	30	31	

November

S	M	T	W	T	F	S
						1
2	3	4	5	6	7	8
9	10	11	12	13	14	15
16	17	18	19	20	21	22
23	24	25	26	27	28	29
30						

December

S	M	T	W	T	F	S
	1	2	3	4	5	6
7	8	9	10	11	12	13
14	15	16	17	18	19	20
21	22	23	24	25	26	27
28	29	30	31			

Important Dates

January

February

March

April

May

June

July

August

September

October

November

December

Birthdays

January	February	March
April	May	June
July	August	September
October	November	December

Projects / Goals / Notes

January 2025

SUNDAY	MONDAY	TUESDAY	WEDNESDAY	THURSDAY
			1	2
5	6	7	8	9
12	13	14	15	16
19	20	21	22	23
26	27	28	29	30

2025

FRIDAY	SATURDAY
3	4
10	11
17	18
24	25
31	

January

SU	MO	TU	WE	TH	FR	SA
			1	2	3	4
5	6	7	8	9	10	11
12	13	14	15	16	17	18
19	20	21	22	23	24	25
26	27	28	29	30	31	

Goals / To Do List

Notes

February 2025

SUNDAY	MONDAY	TUESDAY	WEDNESDAY	THURSDAY
2	3	4	5	6
9	10	11	12	13
16	17	18	19	20
23	24	25	26	27

2025

FRIDAY	SATURDAY
	1
7	8
14	15
21	22
28	

February

SU	MO	TU	WE	TH	FR	SA
						1
2	3	4	5	6	7	8
9	10	11	12	13	14	15
16	17	18	19	20	21	22
23	24	25	26	27	28	

Goals / To Do List

Notes

March 2025

SUNDAY	MONDAY	TUESDAY	WEDNESDAY	THURSDAY
30	31			
2	3	4	5	6
9	10	11	12	13
16	17	18	19	20
23	24	25	26	27

2025

FRIDAY	SATURDAY
	1
7	8
14	15
21	22
28	29

March

SU	MO	TU	WE	TH	FR	SA
						1
2	3	4	5	6	7	8
9	10	11	12	13	14	15
16	17	18	19	20	21	22
23	24	25	26	27	28	29
30	31					

Goals / To Do List

Notes

April 2025

SUNDAY	MONDAY	TUESDAY	WEDNESDAY	THURSDAY
		1	2	3
6	7	8	9	10
13	14	15	16	17
20	21	22	23	24
27	28	29	30	

2025

FRIDAY	SATURDAY
4	5
11	12
18	19
25	26

April

SU	MO	TU	WE	TH	FR	SA
		1	2	3	4	5
6	7	8	9	10	11	12
13	14	15	16	17	18	19
20	21	22	23	24	25	26
27	28	29	30			

Goals / To Do List

Notes

May 2025

SUNDAY	MONDAY	TUESDAY	WEDNESDAY	THURSDAY
				1
4	5	6	7	8
11	12	13	14	15
18	19	20	21	22
25	26	27	28	29

2025

FRIDAY	SATURDAY
2	3
9	10
16	17
23	24
30	31

May

SU	MO	TU	WE	TH	FR	SA
				1	2	3
4	5	6	7	8	9	10
11	12	13	14	15	16	17
18	19	20	21	22	23	24
25	26	27	28	29	30	31

Goals / To Do List

Notes

June 2025

SUNDAY	MONDAY	TUESDAY	WEDNESDAY	THURSDAY
1	2	3	4	5
8	9	10	11	12
15	16	17	18	19
22	23	24	25	26
29	30			

2025

FRIDAY	SATURDAY
6	7
13	14
20	21
27	28

June

SU	MO	TU	WE	TH	FR	SA
1	2	3	4	5	6	7
8	9	10	11	12	13	14
15	16	17	18	19	20	21
22	23	24	25	26	27	28
29	30					

Goals / To Do List

Notes

July 2025

SUNDAY	MONDAY	TUESDAY	WEDNESDAY	THURSDAY
		1	2	3
6	7	8	9	10
13	14	15	16	17
20	21	22	23	24
27	28	29	30	31

2025

FRIDAY	SATURDAY
4	5
11	12
18	19
25	26

July

SU	MO	TU	WE	TH	FR	SA
		1	2	3	4	5
6	7	8	9	10	11	12
13	14	15	16	17	18	19
20	21	22	23	24	25	26
27	28	29	30	31		

Goals / To Do List

Notes

August 2025

SUNDAY	MONDAY	TUESDAY	WEDNESDAY	THURSDAY
31				
3	4	5	6	7
10	11	12	13	14
17	18	19	20	21
24	25	26	27	28

2025

FRIDAY	SATURDAY
1	2
8	9
15	16
22	23
29	30

August

SU	MO	TU	WE	TH	FR	SA
					1	2
3	4	5	6	7	8	9
10	11	12	13	14	15	16
17	18	19	20	21	22	23
24	25	26	27	28	29	30
31						

Goals / To Do List

Notes

September 2025

SUNDAY	MONDAY	TUESDAY	WEDNESDAY	THURSDAY
	1	2	3	4
7	8	9	10	11
14	15	16	17	18
21	22	23	24	25
28	29	30		

2025

FRIDAY	SATURDAY
5	6
12	13
19	20
26	27

September

SU	MO	TU	WE	TH	FR	SA
	1	2	3	4	5	6
7	8	9	10	11	12	13
14	15	16	17	18	19	20
21	22	23	24	25	26	27
28	29	30				

Goals / To Do List

Notes

October 2025

SUNDAY	MONDAY	TUESDAY	WEDNESDAY	THURSDAY
			1	2
5	6	7	8	9
12	13	14	15	16
19	20	21	22	23
26	27	28	29	30

2025

FRIDAY	SATURDAY
3	4
10	11
17	18
24	25
31	

October

SU	MO	TU	WE	TH	FR	SA
			1	2	3	4
5	6	7	8	9	10	11
12	13	14	15	16	17	18
19	20	21	22	23	24	25
26	27	28	29	30	31	

Goals / To Do List

Notes

November 2025

SUNDAY	MONDAY	TUESDAY	WEDNESDAY	THURSDAY
30				
2	3	4	5	6
9	10	11	12	13
16	17	18	19	20
23	24	25	26	27

2025

FRIDAY	SATURDAY
	1
7	8
14	15
21	22
28	29

November

SU	MO	TU	WE	TH	FR	SA
						1
2	3	4	5	6	7	8
9	10	11	12	13	14	15
16	17	18	19	20	21	22
23	24	25	26	27	28	29
30						

Goals / To Do List

- ○ ____
- ○ ____
- ○ ____
- ○ ____
- ○ ____
- ○ ____
- ○ ____
- ○ ____
- ○ ____
- ○ ____
- ○ ____

Notes

December 2025

SUNDAY	MONDAY	TUESDAY	WEDNESDAY	THURSDAY
	1	2	3	4
7	8	9	10	11
14	15	16	17	18
21	22	23	24	25
28	29	30	31	

2025

FRIDAY	SATURDAY
5	6
12	13
19	20
26	27

December

SU	MO	TU	WE	TH	FR	SA
	1	2	3	4	5	6
7	8	9	10	11	12	13
14	15	16	17	18	19	20
21	22	23	24	25	26	27
28	29	30	31			

Goals / To Do List

Notes

NOTES

NOTES

NOTES

NOTES

Full Year at a Glance 2026

January

S	M	T	W	T	F	S
				1	2	3
4	5	6	7	8	9	10
11	12	13	14	15	16	17
18	19	20	21	22	23	24
25	26	27	28	29	30	31

February

S	M	T	W	T	F	S
1	2	3	4	5	6	7
8	9	10	11	12	13	14
15	16	17	18	19	20	21
22	23	24	25	26	27	28

March

S	M	T	W	T	F	S
1	2	3	4	5	6	7
8	9	10	11	12	13	14
15	16	17	18	19	20	21
22	23	24	25	26	27	28
29	30	31				

April

S	M	T	W	T	F	S
			1	2	3	4
5	6	7	8	9	10	11
12	13	14	15	16	17	18
19	20	21	22	23	24	25
26	27	28	29	30		

May

S	M	T	W	T	F	S
					1	2
3	4	5	6	7	8	9
10	11	12	13	14	15	16
17	18	19	20	21	22	23
24	25	26	27	28	29	30
31						

June

S	M	T	W	T	F	S
	1	2	3	4	5	6
7	8	9	10	11	12	13
14	15	16	17	18	19	20
21	22	23	24	25	26	27
28	29	30				

July

S	M	T	W	T	F	S
			1	2	3	4
5	6	7	8	9	10	11
12	13	14	15	16	17	18
19	20	21	22	23	24	25
26	27	28	29	30	31	

August

S	M	T	W	T	F	S
						1
2	3	4	5	6	7	8
9	10	11	12	13	14	15
16	17	18	19	20	21	22
23	24	25	26	27	28	29
30	31					

September

S	M	T	W	T	F	S
		1	2	3	4	5
6	7	8	9	10	11	12
13	14	15	16	17	18	19
20	21	22	23	24	25	26
27	28	29	30			

October

S	M	T	W	T	F	S
				1	2	3
4	5	6	7	8	9	10
11	12	13	14	15	16	17
18	19	20	21	22	23	24
25	26	27	28	29	30	31

November

S	M	T	W	T	F	S
1	2	3	4	5	6	7
8	9	10	11	12	13	14
15	16	17	18	19	20	21
22	23	24	25	26	27	28
29	30					

December

S	M	T	W	T	F	S
		1	2	3	4	5
6	7	8	9	10	11	12
13	14	15	16	17	18	19
20	21	22	23	24	25	26
27	28	29	30	31		

Important Dates

January

February

March

April

May

June

July

August

September

October

November

December

Birthdays

January	February	March

April	May	June

July	August	September

October	November	December

Projects / Goals / Notes

January 2026

SUNDAY	MONDAY	TUESDAY	WEDNESDAY	THURSDAY
				1
4	5	6	7	8
11	12	13	14	15
18	19	20	21	22
25	26	27	28	29

2026

FRIDAY	SATURDAY
2	3
9	10
16	17
23	24
30	31

January

SU	MO	TU	WE	TH	FR	SA
				1	2	3
4	5	6	7	8	9	10
11	12	13	14	15	16	17
18	19	20	21	22	23	24
25	26	27	28	29	30	31

Goals / To Do List

- ○
- ○
- ○
- ○
- ○
- ○
- ○
- ○
- ○
- ○
- ○

Notes

February 2026

SUNDAY	MONDAY	TUESDAY	WEDNESDAY	THURSDAY
1	2	3	4	5
8	9	10	11	12
15	16	17	18	19
22	23	24	25	26

2026

FRIDAY	SATURDAY
6	7
13	14
20	21
27	28

February

SU	MO	TU	WE	TH	FR	SA
1	2	3	4	5	6	7
8	9	10	11	12	13	14
15	16	17	18	19	20	21
22	23	24	25	26	27	28

Goals / To Do List

Notes

March 2026

SUNDAY	MONDAY	TUESDAY	WEDNESDAY	THURSDAY
1	2	3	4	5
8	9	10	11	12
15	16	17	18	19
22	23	24	25	26
29	30	31		

2026

FRIDAY	SATURDAY
6	7
13	14
20	21
27	28

March

SU	MO	TU	WE	TH	FR	SA
1	2	3	4	5	6	7
8	9	10	11	12	13	14
15	16	17	18	19	20	21
22	23	24	25	26	27	28
29	30	31				

Goals / To Do List

Notes

April 2026

SUNDAY	MONDAY	TUESDAY	WEDNESDAY	THURSDAY
			1	2
5	6	7	8	9
12	13	14	15	16
19	20	21	22	23
26	27	28	29	30

2026

FRIDAY	SATURDAY
3	4
10	11
17	18
24	25

April

SU	MO	TU	WE	TH	FR	SA
			1	2	3	4
5	6	7	8	9	10	11
12	13	14	15	16	17	18
19	20	21	22	23	24	25
26	27	28	29	30		

Goals / To Do List

- ○ ______
- ○ ______
- ○ ______
- ○ ______
- ○ ______
- ○ ______
- ○ ______
- ○ ______
- ○ ______
- ○ ______
- ○ ______

Notes

May 2026

SUNDAY	MONDAY	TUESDAY	WEDNESDAY	THURSDAY
31				
3	4	5	6	7
10	11	12	13	14
17	18	19	20	21
24	25	26	27	28

2026

FRIDAY	SATURDAY
1	2
8	9
15	16
22	23
29	30

May

SU	MO	TU	WE	TH	FR	SA
					1	2
3	4	5	6	7	8	9
10	11	12	13	14	15	16
17	18	19	20	21	22	23
24	25	26	27	28	29	30
31						

Goals / To Do List

Notes

June 2026

SUNDAY	MONDAY	TUESDAY	WEDNESDAY	THURSDAY
	1	2	3	4
7	8	9	10	11
14	15	16	17	18
21	22	23	24	25
28	29	30		

2026

FRIDAY	SATURDAY
5	6
12	13
19	20
26	27

June

SU	MO	TU	WE	TH	FR	SA
	1	2	3	4	5	6
7	8	9	10	11	12	13
14	15	16	17	18	19	20
21	22	23	24	25	26	27
28	29	30				

Goals / To Do List

Notes

July 2026

SUNDAY	MONDAY	TUESDAY	WEDNESDAY	THURSDAY
			1	2
5	6	7	8	9
12	13	14	15	16
19	20	21	22	23
26	27	28	29	30

2026

FRIDAY	SATURDAY
3	4
10	11
17	18
24	25
31	

July

SU	MO	TU	WE	TH	FR	SA
			1	2	3	4
5	6	7	8	9	10	11
12	13	14	15	16	17	18
19	20	21	22	23	24	25
26	27	28	29	30	31	

Goals / To Do List

Notes

August 2026

SUNDAY	MONDAY	TUESDAY	WEDNESDAY	THURSDAY
30	31			
2	3	4	5	6
9	10	11	12	13
16	17	18	19	20
23	24	25	26	27

2026

FRIDAY	SATURDAY
	1
7	8
14	15
21	22
28	29

August

SU	MO	TU	WE	TH	FR	SA
						1
2	3	4	5	6	7	8
9	10	11	12	13	14	15
16	17	18	19	20	21	22
23	24	25	26	27	28	29
30	31					

Goals / To Do List

Notes

September 2026

SUNDAY	MONDAY	TUESDAY	WEDNESDAY	THURSDAY
		1	2	3
6	7	8	9	10
13	14	15	16	17
20	21	22	23	24
27	28	29	30	

2026

FRIDAY	SATURDAY
4	5
11	12
18	19
25	26

September

SU	MO	TU	WE	TH	FR	SA
		1	2	3	4	5
6	7	8	9	10	11	12
13	14	15	16	17	18	19
20	21	22	23	24	25	26
27	28	29	30			

Goals / To Do List

Notes

October 2026

SUNDAY	MONDAY	TUESDAY	WEDNESDAY	THURSDAY
				1
4	5	6	7	8
11	12	13	14	15
18	19	20	21	22
25	26	27	28	29

2026

FRIDAY	SATURDAY
2	3
9	10
16	17
23	24
30	31

October

SU	MO	TU	WE	TH	FR	SA
				1	2	3
4	5	6	7	8	9	10
11	12	13	14	15	16	17
18	19	20	21	22	23	24
25	26	27	28	29	30	31

Goals / To Do List

Notes

November 2026

SUNDAY	MONDAY	TUESDAY	WEDNESDAY	THURSDAY
1	2	3	4	5
8	9	10	11	12
15	16	17	18	19
22	23	24	25	26
29	30			

2026

FRIDAY	SATURDAY
6	7
13	14
20	21
27	28

November

SU	MO	TU	WE	TH	FR	SA
1	2	3	4	5	6	7
8	9	10	11	12	13	14
15	16	17	18	19	20	21
22	23	24	25	26	27	28
29	30					

Goals / To Do List

Notes

December 2026

SUNDAY	MONDAY	TUESDAY	WEDNESDAY	THURSDAY
		1	2	3
6	7	8	9	10
13	14	15	16	17
20	21	22	23	24
27	28	29	30	31

2026

FRIDAY	SATURDAY
4	5
11	12
18	19
25	26

December

SU	MO	TU	WE	TH	FR	SA
		1	2	3	4	5
6	7	8	9	10	11	12
13	14	15	16	17	18	19
20	21	22	23	24	25	26
27	28	29	30	31		

Goals / To Do List

Notes

NOTES

NOTES

NOTES

NOTES

Full Year at a Glance 2027

January

S	M	T	W	T	F	S
					1	2
3	4	5	6	7	8	9
10	11	12	13	14	15	16
17	18	19	20	21	22	23
24	25	26	27	28	29	30
31						

February

S	M	T	W	T	F	S
	1	2	3	4	5	6
7	8	9	10	11	12	13
14	15	16	17	18	19	20
21	22	23	24	25	26	27
28						

March

S	M	T	W	T	F	S
	1	2	3	4	5	6
7	8	9	10	11	12	13
14	15	16	17	18	19	20
21	22	23	24	25	26	27
28	29	30	31			

April

S	M	T	W	T	F	S
				1	2	3
4	5	6	7	8	9	10
11	12	13	14	15	16	17
18	19	20	21	22	23	24
25	26	27	28	29	30	

May

S	M	T	W	T	F	S
						1
2	3	4	5	6	7	8
9	10	11	12	13	14	15
16	17	18	19	20	21	22
23	24	25	26	27	28	29
30	31					

June

S	M	T	W	T	F	S
		1	2	3	4	5
6	7	8	9	10	11	12
13	14	15	16	17	18	19
20	21	22	23	24	25	26
27	28	29	30			

July

S	M	T	W	T	F	S
				1	2	3
4	5	6	7	8	9	10
11	12	13	14	15	16	17
18	19	20	21	22	23	24
25	26	27	28	29	30	31

August

S	M	T	W	T	F	S
1	2	3	4	5	6	7
8	9	10	11	12	13	14
15	16	17	18	19	20	21
22	23	24	25	26	27	28
29	30	31				

September

S	M	T	W	T	F	S
			1	2	3	4
5	6	7	8	9	10	11
12	13	14	15	16	17	18
19	20	21	22	23	24	25
26	27	28	29	30		

October

S	M	T	W	T	F	S
					1	2
3	4	5	6	7	8	9
10	11	12	13	14	15	16
17	18	19	20	21	22	23
24	25	26	27	28	29	30
31						

November

S	M	T	W	T	F	S
	1	2	3	4	5	6
7	8	9	10	11	12	13
14	15	16	17	18	19	20
21	22	23	24	25	26	27
28	29	30				

December

S	M	T	W	T	F	S
			1	2	3	4
5	6	7	8	9	10	11
12	13	14	15	16	17	18
19	20	21	22	23	24	25
26	27	28	29	30	31	

Important Dates

January

February

March

April

May

June

July

August

September

October

November

December

Birthdays

January	February	March
April	**May**	**June**
July	**August**	**September**
October	**November**	**December**

Projects / Goals / Notes

January 2027

SUNDAY	MONDAY	TUESDAY	WEDNESDAY	THURSDAY
31				
3	4	5	6	7
10	11	12	13	14
17	18	19	20	21
24	25	26	27	28

2027

FRIDAY	SATURDAY
1	2
8	9
15	16
22	23
29	30

January

SU	MO	TU	WE	TH	FR	SA
					1	2
3	4	5	6	7	8	9
10	11	12	13	14	15	16
17	18	19	20	21	22	23
24	25	26	27	28	29	30
31						

Goals / To Do List

Notes

February 2027

SUNDAY	MONDAY	TUESDAY	WEDNESDAY	THURSDAY
	1	2	3	4
7	8	9	10	11
14	15	16	17	18
21	22	23	24	25
28				

2027

FRIDAY	SATURDAY
5	6
12	13
19	20
26	27

February

SU	MO	TU	WE	TH	FR	SA
	1	2	3	4	5	6
7	8	9	10	11	12	13
14	15	16	17	18	19	20
21	22	23	24	25	26	27
28						

Goals / To Do List

Notes

March 2027

SUNDAY	MONDAY	TUESDAY	WEDNESDAY	THURSDAY
	1	2	3	4
7	8	9	10	11
14	15	16	17	18
21	22	23	24	25
28	29	30	31	

2027

FRIDAY	SATURDAY
5	6
12	13
19	20
26	27

March

SU	MO	TU	WE	TH	FR	SA
	1	2	3	4	5	6
7	8	9	10	11	12	13
14	15	16	17	18	19	20
21	22	23	24	25	26	27
28	29	30	31			

Goals / To Do List

Notes

April 2027

SUNDAY	MONDAY	TUESDAY	WEDNESDAY	THURSDAY
				1
4	5	6	7	8
11	12	13	14	15
18	19	20	21	22
25	26	27	28	29

2027

FRIDAY	SATURDAY
2	3
9	10
16	17
23	24
30	

April

SU	MO	TU	WE	TH	FR	SA
				1	2	3
4	5	6	7	8	9	10
11	12	13	14	15	16	17
18	19	20	21	22	23	24
25	26	27	28	29	30	

Goals / To Do List

Notes

May 2027

SUNDAY	MONDAY	TUESDAY	WEDNESDAY	THURSDAY
30	31			
2	3	4	5	6
9	10	11	12	13
16	17	18	19	20
23	24	25	26	27

2027

FRIDAY	SATURDAY
	1
7	8
14	15
21	22
28	29

May

SU	MO	TU	WE	TH	FR	SA
						1
2	3	4	5	6	7	8
9	10	11	12	13	14	15
16	17	18	19	20	21	22
23	24	25	26	27	28	29
30	31					

Goals / To Do List

Notes

June 2027

SUNDAY	MONDAY	TUESDAY	WEDNESDAY	THURSDAY
		1	2	3
6	7	8	9	10
13	14	15	16	17
20	21	22	23	24
27	28	29	30	

2027

FRIDAY	SATURDAY
4	5
11	12
18	19
25	26

June

SU	MO	TU	WE	TH	FR	SA
		1	2	3	4	5
6	7	8	9	10	11	12
13	14	15	16	17	18	19
20	21	22	23	24	25	26
27	28	29	30			

Goals / To Do List

Notes

July 2027

SUNDAY	MONDAY	TUESDAY	WEDNESDAY	THURSDAY
				1
4	5	6	7	8
11	12	13	14	15
18	19	20	21	22
25	26	27	28	29

2027

FRIDAY	SATURDAY
2	3
9	10
16	17
23	24
30	31

July

SU	MO	TU	WE	TH	FR	SA
				1	2	3
4	5	6	7	8	9	10
11	12	13	14	15	16	17
18	19	20	21	22	23	24
25	26	27	28	29	30	31

Goals / To Do List

Notes

August 2027

SUNDAY	MONDAY	TUESDAY	WEDNESDAY	THURSDAY
1	2	3	4	5
8	9	10	11	12
15	16	17	18	19
22	23	24	25	26
29	30	31		

2027

FRIDAY	SATURDAY
6	7
13	14
20	21
27	28

August

SU	MO	TU	WE	TH	FR	SA
1	2	3	4	5	6	7
8	9	10	11	12	13	14
15	16	17	18	19	20	21
22	23	24	25	26	27	28
29	30	31				

Goals / To Do List

Notes

September 2027

SUNDAY	MONDAY	TUESDAY	WEDNESDAY	THURSDAY
			1	2
5	6	7	8	9
12	13	14	15	16
19	20	21	22	23
26	27	28	29	30

2027

FRIDAY	SATURDAY
3	4
10	11
17	18
24	25

September

SU	MO	TU	WE	TH	FR	SA
			1	2	3	4
5	6	7	8	9	10	11
12	13	14	15	16	17	18
19	20	21	22	23	24	25
26	27	28	29	30		

Goals / To Do List

Notes

October 2027

SUNDAY	MONDAY	TUESDAY	WEDNESDAY	THURSDAY
31				
3	4	5	6	7
10	11	12	13	14
17	18	19	20	21
24	25	26	27	28

2027

FRIDAY	SATURDAY
1	2
8	9
15	16
22	23
29	30

October

SU	MO	TU	WE	TH	FR	SA
					1	2
3	4	5	6	7	8	9
10	11	12	13	14	15	16
17	18	19	20	21	22	23
24	25	26	27	28	29	30
31						

Goals / To Do List

Notes

November 2027

SUNDAY	MONDAY	TUESDAY	WEDNESDAY	THURSDAY
	1	2	3	4
7	8	9	10	11
14	15	16	17	18
21	22	23	24	25
28	29	30		

2027

FRIDAY	SATURDAY
5	6
12	13
19	20
26	27

November

SU	MO	TU	WE	TH	FR	SA
	1	2	3	4	5	6
7	8	9	10	11	12	13
14	15	16	17	18	19	20
21	22	23	24	25	26	27
28	29	30				

Goals / To Do List

Notes

December 2027

SUNDAY	MONDAY	TUESDAY	WEDNESDAY	THURSDAY
			1	2
5	6	7	8	9
12	13	14	15	16
19	20	21	22	23
26	27	28	29	30

2027

FRIDAY	SATURDAY
3	4
10	11
17	18
24	25
31	

December

SU	MO	TU	WE	TH	FR	SA
			1	2	3	4
5	6	7	8	9	10	11
12	13	14	15	16	17	18
19	20	21	22	23	24	25
26	27	28	29	30	31	

Goals / To Do List

Notes

NOTES

NOTES

NOTES

NOTES

Important Contacts

Name: ______________________
Address: ______________________
Phone: ______________________
Notes: ______________________
____

Name: ______________________
Address: ______________________
Phone: ______________________
Notes: ______________________
____

Name: ______________________
Address: ______________________
Phone: ______________________
Notes: ______________________
____

Name: ______________________
Address: ______________________
Phone: ______________________
Notes: ______________________
____

Name: ______________________
Address: ______________________
Phone: ______________________
Notes: ______________________
____

Name: ______________________
Address: ______________________
Phone: ______________________
Notes: ______________________
____

Name: ______________________
Address: ______________________
Phone: ______________________
Notes: ______________________
____

Name: ______________________
Address: ______________________
Phone: ______________________
Notes: ______________________
____

Name: ______________________
Address: ______________________
Phone: ______________________
Notes: ______________________
____

Name: ______________________
Address: ______________________
Phone: ______________________
Notes: ______________________
____

Important Contacts

Name: ______________________
Address: ______________________
Phone: ______________________
Notes: ______________________
____

Name: ______________________
Address: ______________________
Phone: ______________________
Notes: ______________________
____

Name: ______________________
Address: ______________________
Phone: ______________________
Notes: ______________________
____

Name: ______________________
Address: ______________________
Phone: ______________________
Notes: ______________________
____

Name: ______________________
Address: ______________________
Phone: ______________________
Notes: ______________________
____

Name: ______________________
Address: ______________________
Phone: ______________________
Notes: ______________________
____

Name: ______________________
Address: ______________________
Phone: ______________________
Notes: ______________________
____

Name: ______________________
Address: ______________________
Phone: ______________________
Notes: ______________________
____

Name: ______________________
Address: ______________________
Phone: ______________________
Notes: ______________________
____

Name: ______________________
Address: ______________________
Phone: ______________________
Notes: ______________________
____

Password Log

Website: ______________________
Username: ______________________
Password: ______________________
Notes: ______________________
____

Website: ______________________
Username: ______________________
Password: ______________________
Notes: ______________________
____

Website: ______________________
Username: ______________________
Password: ______________________
Notes: ______________________
____

Website: ______________________
Username: ______________________
Password: ______________________
Notes: ______________________
____

Website: ______________________
Username: ______________________
Password: ______________________
Notes: ______________________
____

Website: ______________________
Username: ______________________
Password: ______________________
Notes: ______________________
____

Website: ______________________
Username: ______________________
Password: ______________________
Notes: ______________________
____

Website: ______________________
Username: ______________________
Password: ______________________
Notes: ______________________
____

Website: ______________________
Username: ______________________
Password: ______________________
Notes: ______________________
____

Website: ______________________
Username: ______________________
Password: ______________________
Notes: ______________________
____

Password Log

Website:

Username:

Password:

Notes:

Website:

Username:

Password:

Notes:

Website:

Username:

Password:

Notes:

Website:

Username:

Password:

Notes:

Website:

Username:

Password:

Notes:

Website:

Username:

Password:

Notes:

Website:

Username:

Password:

Notes:

Website:

Username:

Password:

Notes:

Website:

Username:

Password:

Notes:

Website:

Username:

Password:

Notes:

Made in United States
North Haven, CT
02 November 2022

26220573R00091